Tried and Tested Strategies: Play and Learning in the Early Years

Tried and Tested Strategies: Play and Learning in the Early Years

An inclusive approach

Angela Glenn,
Jacquie Cousins and
Alicia Helps

David Fulton Publishers

David Fulton Publishers Ltd
The Chiswick Centre, 414 Chiswick High Road, London W4 5TF

www.fultonpublishers.co.uk

David Fulton Publishers is a division of Granada Learning Limited, part of ITV plc.

10 9 8 7 6 5 4 3 2 1

British Library Cataloguing in Publication Data
A catalogue record for this book is available from the British Library.

ISBN: 1 84312 336 3

Typeset by Servis Filmsetting Ltd, Manchester
Printed and bound in Great Britain

CONTENTS

ACKNOWLEDGEMENTS

We would like to thank John, Victoria and Sarah for their encouragement.

We would also like to thank colleagues in the Medway Pre-schools for being so welcoming and for demonstrating such commitment and passion to early years education.

Thanks to all the staff at David Fulton Publishers, especially to Linda Evans.

Thank you to Jacey Abram for doing the illustrations.

INTRODUCTION

Play is the principal means of learning in the early years. Young children learn most effectively through personal experiences and a multisensory teaching approach that taps into their natural sense of curiosity. Play, in all its many guises, presents endless opportunities for children to interact with people and objects in both real and imaginary situations, and should be central to the planning of a Foundation Stage curriculum.

   A good practitioner will be open to picking up on children's interests and making the curriculum fit the child rather than the other way around. The information on page 25 of the *Curriculum Guidance for the Foundation Stage* (QCA 2000) sets out some key principles. Children can:

- explore, develop and represent learning experiences that help them make sense of the world
- practise and build up ideas, concepts and skills
- learn how to control impulses and understand the need for rules
- be alone, be alongside others or co-operate as they talk or rehearse their feelings

- take risks and make mistakes
- think creatively and imaginatively
- communicate with others as they investigate or solve problems
- express fears or relive anxious experiences in controlled and safe situations

In today's world, there is much emphasis upon assessing, recording, monitoring and testing. Practitioners spend vast amounts of time engaged in ticking boxes and filling out observations (which, by the way, are mostly descriptions of what children are doing rather than the focused kind of observation which informs). Children deserve the enthusiastic engagement and interaction of a practitioner who helps them to build upon what they already know and teaches and inspires them to want to know more.

This book begins with a brief section (Section 1) about the theories of play, involving parents and about how play can help children with emotional difficulties. The case studies in Section 2 reflect some of the ways in which children present and ideas about how to help them. In view of the ever-increasing number of children who lack play skills in the early years and who are referred to Behaviour Outreach Teams, we thought that this may be of value to practitioners who would like to do something practical (and enjoyable!) in this area. The book follows on with ideas to support children's learning (Section 3) and suggestions for providing a suitable learning environment (Section 4).

These days, it seems that children spend the larger part of their lives either inside their houses, inside other people's houses or inside shops. There seems to be a real reluctance on the part of parents to allow their children much outdoor freedom at all. Most children are driven to and from school even if they live very close by. Although this is understandable on one level, it can limit a child's development. In view of this, it is all the more important that pre-schools and schools provide an outdoor space for learning and discovery.

There is no substitute for playing outdoors. Children who have regular access to an outdoor area will be healthier, happier, learn from their environment and be less stressed. It is difficult to replicate outdoor activities indoors, and it is impossible to replicate the feeling of freedom and the exploration the outdoor environment can provide. The development of gross motor skills is an essential building block for future learning and this can best be practised outdoors on large apparatus.

The ideal early years setting is a free flowing, high quality, carefully planned and structured, play-orientated learning environment, indoors and out. Children are far more likely to learn concepts such as colour by looking at plants and animals during an exciting fact-finding exercise outside. The child who is reluctant to engage in pencil and paper activities may well be more engaged when asked to dig up the longest worm or to find the smallest snail!

SECTION 1

The importance of play

Theories of play

Involving parents

Using play to help children with emotional difficulties

Learning through play

Theories of play

Imagine a typical scene of a group of children in the kitchen. The first is 18 months old and has a saucepan. He has managed to find a wooden spoon and is 'making cakes'. Another child is sitting on the floor with her dolls reading them a story. The third is sitting at a table, has found two spoons and is banging them together saying, 'I'm a pop star.'

Throughout the ages healthy children have found opportunities to play but this activity has not always been recognised for its value. The following are a few of the major theories that have been put forward over the years to attempt to explain children's play.

Evolutionary theory

In the nineteenth century, the evolutionary theory gave a tremendous insight into child development and an impetus to the study of this area. An interest in the development of infants from other species led to an interest in the newborn baby and how children learn to become adults. Play was carefully observed and became regarded as essential practice at becoming an adult through role play. This can be seen as children copy a range of activities and behaviours demonstrated by adults in games such as 'playing mummies and daddies' in the home corner and 'playing teachers'.

Practice of skills for survival

This theory puts emphasis on the practice of skills for survival. It emphasises play as practising and perfecting the skills needed for later life. As with the previous theory, this idea arose from animal studies where young animals were observed constantly play-fighting in preparation for their self-preservation in later life.

In human child development this can be seen in such areas as children learning to share or to take turns and in their attempting to resolve disputes. These are all skills that will be necessary for these individuals to fully take part in the social organisations of life, such as school, work and family.

Play as an attitude

Play is usually connected with laughter and fun and is regarded as a pleasurable activity. Children can become totally absorbed in an activity which really interests them. This theory was that play is a state of mind and stems from absorption in that pleasurable activity.

We can see this when we observe children who appear to be totally involved in their role play. Any pre-school observation will include children who are in the dressing-up corner and have 'become' a fireman or a shopkeeper. Similarly, many children become completely involved with cause-and-effect toys, especially musical toys, and will play with these toys time and time again.

Play and the growth of intelligence

A further theory was put forward by Piaget, who carefully observed children's early development. Originally a zoologist, Piaget's ideas have been highly influential in the field of child development. Piaget hypothesised that play was closely bound up with the growth of intelligence. He spoke of two processes that he believed were fundamental to all development: 'assimilation' and 'accommodation', which basically mean taking things in and making sense and use of them.

Piaget spoke of the constant interplay needed between these two processes for effective learning. A child always tries to make sense of the information they receive and tries to relate it to something they already know.

When these two processes are not in balance, Piaget commented that this results in imitation. This can occur because the child is confused and the child is trying to understand the situation in the best way he or she knows how. Children who play at the same game or the same role play time and time again based on something they have seen could be imitating.

Assimilation is the child's way of making sense of the information. It results in play where the child is playing with the information they have in order to make sense of it.

Play as a means of working through emotions

The famous psychoanalyst, Freud, drew attention to the fact that children learn to work through their emotions through play. Children can safely work through a range of emotions through role play or by acting out a story. Puppets can be very useful in situations where a child finds it easier to express his or her feelings through a different character.

Today's practitioners understand that play serves a range of functions at different stages of a child's social, emotional, behavioural and intellectual development and makes a vital contribution to preparing them for adulthood.

Involving parents

Early years practitioners have an important role to play in sharing their knowledge about the importance of play with parents and carers and offering suggestions about how learning can be supported at home. Parents want to give their children the best start in life and can be vulnerable to advertising on television and in magazines for so-called 'educational' toys. These can be expensive, and are often no more than gimmicks. More often than not, more valuable learning experiences can be provided at little or no cost in the home. It always amazes parents when their child receives a present and shows more interest in the cardboard box container than in its contents. The box represents a stimulus to the child's imagination: it can become a car, a spaceship, a boat, a house.

Keeping parents informed about what is going on in the setting and particular topics being covered can give them ideas for activities. A regular information sheet can help – though take care not to bombard families with too much paper! (See pp. 5–6 for a sample newsletter.)

There are several ways that parents can be encouraged to share in their child's play activities. For example:

- Parent and toddler groups invite parents to share in play activities with their children. These can be art and craft activities, play with construction toys, sharing books or simply talking with children about what is happening. For example, making bread or playing with playdough can encourage a richness of language and also develop creative and imaginary thinking.

- Some pre-schools use parents as voluntary helpers for specific sessions. These sessions are usually as much fun for the parents as for the children. They can provide a valuable opportunity for parents to see how fun equipment can be used in small areas. For example, a small tray of sand and a bowl of water with a plastic mat underneath could be used in the home or in the garden. Household items such as spoons, plastic cups and other household utensils can provide a rich practical experience for children where parents can add the language to support the child's development of mathematical and scientific concepts such as 'heavier', 'sinking' or 'how many?'.

- It is important that parents who find it difficult to play with their children are shown good role models. Pre-school staff will need to praise the child for the activities they are carrying out and demonstrate how effective praise can be in encouraging children to develop play and concentrate on activities. For some parents it may become a different way of viewing their child when they see the child's responses.

- Increasingly, toy libraries are being set up in children's centres. If a child in pre-school or at a childminder's shows an interest in a particular toy it may be possible to borrow that toy or a similar toy from a toy library.

- There are a number of different schemes that have been set up to encourage parents and children to play together. In some cases a professional comes into the family home and plays with the child (either with the child's own toys or with toys they take into the home) to model appropriate activities. Other schemes encourage parents to meet in family-friendly places where a range of fun activities have been set up. (Details of these schemes can be found through local children's information services.) These are valuable in demonstrating a variety of games to parents and extending their 'repertoire' of things to do with their children. (See pp. 5–6 for some suggestions of games to play with children.)

- In many pre-schools the outdoor play is becoming increasingly important because professionals recognise that children engage and learn most effectively in natural settings. Parents can often be encouraged to view or accompany some outdoor activities, then replicate the activities at home. A walk to the local shops can initiate making a shopping list, deciding

First Steps Nursery

'Growth and Living Things'

Dear Parents and Carers,

Now that spring is with us, we will be looking particularly at 'growth and living things' with the children. We have planned some exciting activities including:

- Observing the life cycle of a butterfly and a frog (caterpillars and frogspawn are due to arrive next week – look out for the 'Living Things' display!).
- A visit to a local farm (parents and carers will be invited to join us – details to follow).
- A search for 'mini-beasts' in the outside play area.
- Growing a range of vegetables and flowers, observing and measuring their growth.
- A visit from a health visitor, talking about keeping healthy.

There are many ways in which you can help to develop your child's learning about 'growth and living things' at home. Here are a few suggestions from us – please let us know about your good ideas so that we can share them with other parents!

- A visit to the park looking at, and talking about, leaves, buds, flowers, insects.
- Making a scrapbook of things found in the park.
- A visit to a local garden centre to look at plants, seedlings, trees, shrubs.
- Digging and planting – there are many plants that will happily grow in pots on a windowsill if access to a garden or 'allotment' is difficult. (Cut-off carrot tops in a saucer of water quickly grow shoots and require little attention!)
- Talking about pets – how they have changed as they have grown, and the care they need.
- Talking about their own growth and the food/care they need to be healthy.
- Looking at photographs of themselves (from babyhood to present day).

Thanks for your co-operation – have fun investigating with your child!

The nursery staff

(*Source:* from Drake (2005) *Planning Children's Play and Learning in the Foundation Stage*)

Games to play

Teddy bears' picnic (or use dolls, puppets, furry animals) Talk about what to take – sandwiches, biscuits, cakes, something to drink. Make the picnic (real or pretend). Spread a cloth – inside or out, in the garden or the park. Hand round the food, 'Would you like a cheese sandwich Teddy?' – saying please and thank you. Talk about food that you like, and don't like. Make sure you tidy up all the litter. Do the washing up together.

Make a camp (or house, cave, spaceship) inside or out. Provide an old blanket or curtain, large sheet of cardboard or box. A clothes-drier frame makes a good framework, or a swing or climbing frame; inside use a table or two chairs. Provide a torch if it is dark inside. Make a bed and seats with cushions and a blanket. Have visitors – make them welcome.

Make playdough Mix the ingredients (1 cup flour, 4 teaspoons salt, 7–8 cups cold water plus a little food colouring) well and store in the fridge. Shape it into different foods, animals or shapes. See who can make the longest 'worm'.

Make cakes using an all-in-one cake mix. (4 oz margarine, 4 oz caster sugar, 2 eggs, 4 oz self-raising flour, 2 oz sultanas or chocolate chips) Put all the ingredients into a bowl and mix well with a wooden spoon until there are no lumps. Spoon the mixture into paper cases on a baking tray and bake at Reg 4 or 180°C for 15–20 minutes. Do the washing up together. (Take care around the cooker – talk about the heat and the need to be careful etc. – adults only to use the oven.)

Shops, post office, café Collect some 'props'. Take it in turns to be the customer and assistant/waiter. Use real or pretend money.

Hide and seek One player covers their eyes and counts to ten – or says a nursery rhyme, or waits for the song to finish, then goes to look for the players who are hiding. The first one to be found has to be the 'finder' next time. Play in the garden, in the house or in the park (if it is safe).

Skittles Make your own with plastic bottles. Use a big ball – roll it, throw it, kick it.

Football Make a goal area and take it in turns to kick the ball into the goal. Make a circle with string, take it in turns to throw in bean bags, shells, pebbles. See who can get the most inside the circle.

Animal capers Take it in turns to shout the name of an animal – everyone has to move and sound like the animal.

Statues Dance/walk/hop/jump to some music or the shaking of a tambourine. When the music stops, everyone has to 'freeze' until the music starts again.

which route to take, having the money and shopping bag ready. Teddy or dolly could also go in a pushchair. The physical exercise involved in outdoor play and walking is an important part of healthy living and should be encouraged.

- Even a very small garden or outdoor area can be used for growing plants, perhaps in pots. Early years settings can encourage this type of activity by demonstrating how to plant seeds, and how to nurture them – perhaps running a competition to see whose plant grows tallest etc.

Using play to help children with emotional difficulties

Most pre-school workers will at some stage experience situations where a child has a bereavement, someone is very ill, or there is some kind of tension in the family home. Occasionally, there may also be concern about a child's safety within the family situation. Many people will be unsure how best they can help the child and also how to help the other children in the pre-school to respond sympathetically. The aim of this part of Section 1 is to help to recognise the emotions these children are likely to be going through and offer some practical support through various play activities.

It is important to note that some children may need highly specialist support in working through their emotional difficulties and it may be possible to link with the specialists involved, possibly an educational psychologist or counsellor, to discuss an appropriate way forward. If there are concerns about safety, then child protection procedures will come into force. With adult support, however, most children can be guided into opportunities to work through their concerns.

One of the most important aspects of the home, childminder or pre-school setting is that the child already has a rapport with the adults and is in a familiar context. Children are far more likely to relax and to share their worries in more familiar settings, with adults in whom they have built up a trust.

Identification

Children show signs of distress in different ways:
- Constant anxiety
- Sudden mood swings
- Lack of concentration
- Crying suddenly, for no obvious reason
- Eating difficulties/disorders
- Acting out sexual behaviour
- A lack of expression

- Unwillingness to return home
- Not willing to play with other children

Any of these behaviours can signal feelings of anger, resentment, grief, betrayal, confusion or self-blame. Children often blame themselves if things are going wrong at home. A comment may be made such as, 'The kids are driving me mad, I can't stand it any more.' A sensitive child could take this comment to heart and blame themselves, especially if it results in arguments between the parents. A child could be faced with a dramatic scene, e.g. Mum or Dad swearing, slamming the door and saying they are leaving. Children become anxious in case the parent does not come back. Security can become a real issue for these children.

If you notice any of the above symptoms, it can be useful to focus on the child's play to see if there are opportunities to support the child. Careful observation could also provide useful information to any specialists who might later need to become involved. Where there is concern, it may be helpful to speak to parents or carers – but great sensitivity and utmost confidentiality need to be employed.

What can help?

Stories

There are many stories now which address issues such as bereavement, separation or a sibling who is different. These stories are probably best read in a group situation so that children can make a range of comments. Initially, a child going through emotional difficulties may find it difficult to express an opinion or make any comments. They may also feel very unsure about their own feelings. Some children are also unlikely to have the vocabulary to express how they feel and storytelling could provide a good opportunity to help the child to put words to the emotions. The child may be helped by listening to the comments and views of other children. This is particularly so if children are involved in the story by asking such questions as, 'How do you think the boy in the story felt?' and possibly, 'Has anyone ever felt like that?'.

The child may offer a response but if they are not ready to join in, they may find it useful to listen to the views of other children. It is also very helpful if the adult can talk about how these feelings are normal.

Useful books for talking about bereavement and loss include:

- *Grandpa and Me* by Alex Marley (ISBN 0 85648 442 3)
- *Goodbye Max* by Holly Keller (ISBN 0 862 03307 1)
- *Emma's Cat Dies* by Nigel Snell (ISBN 0 241 11297 4)
- *Badger's Parting Gift* by Susan Varley (ISBN 0 862 64062 8)

Advice and resources on bereavement can be obtained from your local branch of Cruse Bereavement Care (see 'Useful addresses' section for contact details).

Dolls' house

A dolls' house with a range of characters can help children to act out situations. Many of the children will act out the same situation time and time again until it makes a little more sense to them. Some children may be helped by having an adult with them, talking through the actions of the dolls and asking what the characters are doing and why. The opportunity to explain that Mummy might have shouted because she was very tired can help a child who feels that he or she is the cause of their parents' anger.

Puppets

By acting out a situation through puppets and dolls the child can put across his or her feelings in a safe way. Puppets can help a child who is very quiet or will not speak to others. Children can project their voices or the personality of someone they know into the puppet or doll. Even if the child does not vocalise they are able to use the puppets or dolls to perform actions and the manner of the actions can often give clues about the child's feelings. It will also be useful to observe how the puppet relates to the other puppets or dolls.

Dressing-up corner

Dressing up allows children to take on different roles and work through anxieties and emotions. For example a child in the role of Daddy may shout and swear a lot, imitating the sort of parental behaviour he sees in the home. Observing this scenario can give early years practitioners a useful insight into family situations – but do be wary of jumping to conclusions; the child may be imitating a scene from a television 'soap' rather than reflecting his own circumstances! Sensitive conversation with the child will establish where he has seen this behaviour.

Children often blame themselves for things that go wrong and the dressing-up area can provide a useful opportunity to act out situations in a safe way or to try out alternative ways of responding to situations.

Drama

Children can listen to a story and then act out the story in the book. Many children's stories can be extended in this way where the children can take on different characters each time. Most children love stories to be repeated. For example, the story of the *Three Little Pigs* could be acted out easily with different children taking on the role of the wolf and the three pigs. Simple costumes could be made by the children. These could be such things as a headband with pink ears for the pigs and a mask for the wolf. There are many tables and stories dealing with specific issues which could be used. The library service is usually very helpful in having lists of suitable books.

Alternatively the children can act out emotions as part of a story, for example, 'Then the farmer got very angry. Let's see if you can look angry like the farmer.' This activity helps children to identify and put a name to their own and other people's feelings. It can also be very reassuring to learn that everybody has similar feelings.

Children can also be encouraged to make up their own stories and choose their own characters. This can be either guided by adults or done independently by the children. Most children happily engage in imaginary activities as a normal part of their learning and development.

Art

Many children find painting and drawing to be a highly stimulating experience. Children will often choose colours of paint that represent the emotions they are feeling, such as red for anger, black for feeling desperate. It is invaluable to enable children to use paints or craft materials in ways that enable them to express their emotions. Some children may do a painting and then cover the whole painting in black or red with thick heavy strokes.

It can be helpful to ask the children to draw specific things on occasions, such as their family or pets or themselves. If a child is able to use drawing or painting as a medium it can be very effective in providing an opportunity to put feelings into a concrete format and opens a way for talking about them.

Art as a therapeutic technique is used by specialists and more information about this can be obtained from The British Association of Art Therapists (see 'Useful addresses' section for contact details).

Games

Some children find it very difficult to share equipment or take turns. Games form a highly structured way of helping to develop these skills. Games such as picture lotto, dominoes and snap are easy to understand and most children enjoy them. An important part of this sort of activity is learning to accept second or third place and coping with not being the winner of a game. Appropriate praise from the adults involved will go a long way to reinforcing appropriate behaviour: 'Well done Maisie, I really like the way you took turns today. And well done Sam for playing so nicely. I really liked the way you waited for Maisie when she was thinking about which card to play.'

Games specifically designed as therapy tools are available from specialist providers such as Smallwood Publishing Ltd (see 'Useful addresses' for contact details).

Large equipment

Some children with emotional and behavioural difficulties benefit from being able to run around and let off steam in a spacious area with large play equipment. These areas need to be carefully thought through so that children can utilise their energy in a safe way. For some children the play equipment may provide the main opportunity to develop gross motor skills and help them to gain confidence in their own ability. It also offers opportunities for them to be 'in the driving seat' in terms of controlling the tricycle or pedal car and can be valuable in building up self-esteem.

Small enclosed spaces

Children often benefit from the opportunity to withdraw when a situation becomes difficult for them. A small tent in a corner of the room could help a child to feel enclosed and secure. It will be important to monitor how such a space is used, for how long and by which children. Frequent use may signal a child who needs some extra attention and support.

Using musical instruments

Musical instruments can help children to express their emotions, especially when they have a limited command of expressive language. Instruments such as drums, triangles, hand chimes and xylophones are popular, but home-made ones can be just as much fun – beans/rice/pebbles in a tin or jar; wooden spoons and a plastic bucket or metal saucepan. They could play happy, sad or angry tunes on their instruments, adopting appropriate facial expressions and perhaps being encouraged to talk about things that make them happy, sad or angry – or point to pictures.

Musical instruments could also be played by children or adults and other children could be encouraged to move or dance to the rhythm. 'Let's move in a happy way. How are we feeling when we are happy?' 'Let's move in an angry way.' This type of activity will help children to recognise their own feelings and put words to how they feel.

Many specialists in children's emotional needs such as child psychologists use various types of play therapy as a medium to allow children to work through their emotions.

The play therapy may be a short-term intervention or a process that extends over a longer period, according to each child's needs. A play therapist helps the child to make sense of their life experiences and to express difficult feelings through the metaphors of play. If children are having specialist therapeutic intervention, try to link with the specialists involved and see if they can offer suggestions that can be carried out in the setting.

Learning through play

Most young children learn easily, through everything they see and hear, touch, taste and smell – but mostly through what they 'do'. For some, however, learning may be problematic, for a variety of reasons. By being aware of the learning gains which can be made in different situations, early years practitioners can take a more pro-active approach in supporting children's learning and minimising any barriers to the development of foundation skills.

The lists of skills learned from different activities shown on pp. 12–14 are not exhaustive, but can be added to by practitioners and used in planning, especially for children who need some extra support.

Sit-on and ride-on toys

- Sharing, taking turns
- Motor skill control
- Exploring movement in space
- Manoeuvring (steering, turning)
- Avoiding collisions – being aware of others
- Experiencing speed
- Decision making, e.g. which way to go, how fast
- Understanding cause and effect

Sand and water play

- Developing ideas about volume and quantity, e.g. more and less, a lot and a little
- Differences between wet and dry sand
- Co-operative digging, playing and building
- Floating and sinking
- Developing fine and gross motor skills
- Sharing equipment

Ball games

- Learning about and accepting rules
- Fair play
- Taking turns
- Following instructions or signals
- Hand–eye co-ordination
- Catching
- Throwing
- Kicking
- Aiming
- Running
- Rolling

Playhouse/shop/café

- Role play, e.g. imitating, using imagination
- Language development, e.g. naming of objects, using appropriate conventions – please and thank you etc.
- Acknowledging needs of others
- Observing and taking part in social practice
- Recognising appropriate dress

Outdoor/indoor garden area

- Observation
- Awareness of cycles in nature
- Living things, e.g. conditions needed for growth, changes
- Measurement
- Artwork
- Language development, e.g. vocabulary, being able to comment and describe
- Appreciation of natural beauty and respect for living creatures

Large apparatus, such as climbing frames

- Awareness of body parts
- Taking weight on different parts of the body
- Co-ordination
- Co-operation
- Learning about and accepting safety rules
- Self-control
- Testing out and developing courage
- Balancing, swinging, sliding and hanging

Daily weather chart

- Observing and commenting on weather conditions
- Noticing effects of weather on play, outings and what to wear

- Experiencing use of simple weather gauges
- Understanding the cycle of the seasons
- Developing an understanding of protection from the weather, e.g. sun screen in summer, warm clothing in cold weather etc.

SECTION 2

Case studies

1. A child who flits from one toy to another
2. A child who is aggressive towards others while playing/interferes with others
3. A child who cannot share
4. A child who uses equipment inappropriately, lines items up, doesn't care for things
5. A child who doesn't play imaginatively
6. A child who doesn't engage in role play
7. A child who is frightened to engage in climbing/physical activities
8. A child who shows no fear or is impulsive
9. A child who avoids toys such as tricycle and scooters
10. A child who refuses to play an adult-led or organised game
11. A child who always plays 'mum' in the home corner
12. A child who refuses to let others play the same 'game' as them
13. A child who cannot accept losing a game (snakes and ladders)
14. A child who cannot play by set rules
15. A child who dislikes playing outside
16. A child who always plays with one particular child
17. A child whose play is repetitive
18. A child who only engages in play if directed by an adult
19. A child who always seeks out (holds the hand of) an adult during outside play sessions
20. A child who becomes upset when faced with unfamiliar situations
21. A child who always plays with 'baby' toys
22. A child who becomes out of control and overexcited during boisterous activity
23. A child who cannot wait for his/her turn
24. A child who cannot adapt to the suggestions of others during games or activities
25. A child who uses a lot of violence in play

CASE STUDY 1

A child who flits from one toy to another

Chloe loves to go to nursery. She runs straight in and quickly goes to the home corner, then runs over to look at the cars and garage. She takes hold of a car and runs with it to the slide. She knocks and bangs the car against the slide and then moves on to the sand. She puts the car in the sand and goes over to the nursery assistant and points outside, indicating she wants to go out and play.

Possible reasons for this behaviour

Chloe:
- has not been taught how to choose activities she is interested in
- is unsure how to develop her play
- needs to develop her concentration skills
- finds the situation overstimulating
- may have generalised learning difficulties or social communication difficulties

Strategies

- Use a High/Scope approach where Chloe chooses two or three activities she will carry out. She may initially need the support of an adult. (For information on the High/Scope approach see Glenn *et al.* (2005) and for contact details of the High/Scope Institute in London see 'Useful addresses' section.)
- Model appropriate play activity for Chloe. Encourage imaginative play and provide language support, e.g. 'Let's take dolly for a walk,' and 'Let's bring dolly back and put her to bed.'
- Support Chloe in playing alongside other children. She should initially be with one child and given a specific short task such as, 'See if you can make a car with Lego.' It will be very important to monitor these types of activities very carefully to gain a deeper understanding of the way Chloe is able to approach tasks
- Chloe may also have restricted language comprehension. It may be useful to use a visual support such as photographs and pictures

CASE STUDY 2

A child who is aggressive towards others while playing/interferes with others

James generally plays on his own in the pre-school. He is at his happiest when he is playing with the building equipment and he has a good imagination. He can build quite elaborate constructions and freely talk about them. Adults constantly praise him for his designs. Problems begin when other children come to play with the construction equipment, especially when one of them builds a good model. James has been seen to break the other child's model and take the pieces he wants. On several occasions he has hit the other child as well, telling them to keep away as he is using the equipment.

Possible reasons for this behaviour

James:
- likes to have sole praise for building nice models. He does not want to see the other child getting praise as well
- knows he is good at making models and does not feel he is good at other things. He wants to feel that making good models is special to him. This is James's way of preserving his self-esteem, which could be very low in other areas
- has not yet learnt to share
- is not used to sharing equipment as he has the construction equipment to himself at home

Strategies

- Encourage James to show other people how he builds things so well and 'help' them to build a model of their own. Initially this could be by 'helping' an adult
- Praise James for effort for other things he does at pre-school. Emphasis should be placed on the importance of trying new things and 'having a go'
- Encourage James to share equipment, initially with one other child. Sharing can be very difficult for some children and at first they will need to be praised for every little act of sharing. Turn-taking activities may help with this where the equipment is initially divided and each person has a turn, e.g. in building a tower of bricks

CASE STUDY 3

A child who cannot share

Cherish really looks forward to pre-school mornings and her mum says she puts her coat on as soon as she gets up! At pre-school Cherish constantly snatches toys from other children and punches children out of the way. Cherish particularly enjoys the slide and finds it difficult to wait for her turn. She pushes children up the steps and down the slide and there have been several accidents. At the table-top activities Cherish sweeps all the toys, crayons etc. up in her arms and says 'it's mine'. Many of the children get very upset and Cherish appears unconcerned by their cries.

Possible reasons for this behaviour

Cherish:
- finds it very difficult to interact socially with other children and understand that they want to play
- holds a high level of control within her family and wants to carry this through into the pre-school setting
- has difficulty with motor skills and her movements appear unco-ordinated and dangerous on occasions

Strategies

- Monitor Cherish's behaviour with other children to determine whether she shows any initiation of interaction. It may be helpful to check with her parents whether this behaviour also happens at home
- Initiate further assessments for any medical condition, such as difficulties with motor skills, hearing, social communication difficulties or difficulties with attention
- Implement a specific programme so that Cherish has some individual time with an adult each session and her rate of learning new tasks can be monitored
- Support her in turn-taking activities in a paired setting so that she recognises she needs to wait for her turn

CASE STUDY 4

A child who uses equipment inappropriately, lines items up, doesn't care for things

Storm's mother often told the pre-school staff how good and quiet he was at home and that he would play happily for hours and 'you wouldn't know he was there'. At pre-school, staff have noted that Storm plays on his own almost all the time. He loves the trains and will sit happily lining them up and then putting them back in the box and then lining them up again. He gets upset if anyone else comes to join in his play. He will then throw the equipment around, usually aiming at the other children. Outdoors, he happily plays with the grit on the pathway. If people come towards him he will often throw the grit at them.

Possible reasons for this behaviour

Storm:
- feels reassured that he has the same equipment at home and at pre-school
- has difficulties with playing imaginatively. He enjoys the security of the toys he is familiar with. This will need to be monitored as it could be indicative of a child with social communication difficulties (and possibly autism)
- has not learnt to share equipment and does not know how to manage when others want to join in with his play
- is a very anxious child

Strategies

- Put specific programmes in place to help Storm to extend his range of activities. He is likely to need adult support to show him how to play with other items of equipment
- Allow Storm to continue with the activities he enjoys but manage these. For example, Storm could be taught a pattern of playing with activities such as 'first painting, then cars'. This would be done through a visual timetable approach so that Storm is familiar with expectations. It will be very important that Storm is allowed the activities he chooses and these could be used as a reward
- Discuss Storm's activities with his parents. He may need further assessment. It will be important to monitor Storm's interaction with other children and also his method of communicating with others

CASE STUDY 5

A child who doesn't play imaginatively

Robert's mother informed pre-school staff that Robert always got fully involved in his play and would play for hours at home with his cars or his toy trains. The pre-school staff noted that this was so and it was difficult to disturb Robert once he had started to play. Robert also enjoyed the home corner and would spend considerable time with the washing machine. When Robert was closely observed, staff noted that Robert would line up his cars very methodically and 'chat' to himself and would then get the cars out again and put them in exactly the same order. This was the same with the trains. In the home corner Robert would fill the washing machine with items of clothing and then take the clothes out in reverse order. He did this several times.

Possible reasons for this behaviour

Robert:
- enjoys the sameness and pattern of activities he chooses
- does these activities at home and replicates them at nursery. In this way he feels secure
- may have hearing or receptive language difficulties or social communication difficulties
- is trying to make sense of events in his life

Strategies

- Engage Robert in a discussion about his cars, trains or clothes and encourage him to allow an adult to share the activity with him. In this way he may start to talk about his play. Should there be any concerns, these could be discussed with Robert's parents or carers
- Invite Robert to choose one car or one item of clothing and use it in a different way, such as using the car with a garage or dressing teddy in the item of clothing
- Take the equipment outside and away from the usual indoor location in the pre-school
- Let a teddy or a puppet join in the play initially to encourage turn taking

CASE STUDY 6

A child who doesn't engage in role play

The school staff enjoy setting up the play situations for their children. In the past they have had a cave, a shop, a train, a circus and a ship among others. Nahrinder cannot understand how anyone can expect that a box with paint on it can be a ship. He tells the other children, 'It is a box, we painted it. It is not a ship.' The other children tell Nahrinder, 'No, it is a ship,' 'Come and be a pirate.' Nahrinder gets very cross and upset and runs to the staff on these occasions.

Possible reasons for this behaviour

Nahrinder:
- has not yet developed skills of imaginative thinking. His skills are very much at the concrete level
- is anxious about imaginary situations
- may have had limited experiences outside of his home
- is encouraged to be 'grown up' at home and feels that pretend play is babyish

Strategies

- Show Nahrinder boats and pictures about the various play situations to see whether he can become involved in the story. He should be asked questions such as, 'What do you think will happen next?' or 'What would happen if . . .?'
- Give Nahrinder opportunities to visit real boats, trains and other experiences. He may not have experienced these situations in real life so may find it very difficult to imagine them and play with them
- Look at books and talk about what is happening in the pictures. Nahrinder could then watch other children acting out stories from books in the first instance. Gradually, he may become involved more and join in
- Act out the stories with Nahrinder using puppets
- Find out from Nahrinder's parents/carers about stories that are part of their cultural tradition and use some of these as a starting point for imaginative play

CASE STUDY 7

A child who is frightened to engage in climbing/physical activities

Hamish watches as the other children have fun on the slides and big equipment. He looks as if he would like to have a go but if an adult or another child approaches him he will just stand there and say, 'No' and will turn his head and body away.

Possible reasons for this behaviour

Hamish may:
- have had a bad experience or fall in the past and is reluctant to try again
- have overprotective parents/carers who are concerned about him engaging in more physical activities
- feel he will fall
- have sensory integration problems
- be dyspraxic or 'clumsy'
- receive more attention if he does not engage in activities and this has developed into a pattern of responding

Strategies

- Talk to Hamish's parents/carers to check whether there are any reasons for Hamish's concern
- Design a programme to help with motor skills development. It would be useful to find out if Hamish has had medical investigations. If not, this could be suggested to parents
- Allow Hamish to play on the equipment when other children are not there, so he gains confidence
- Give him lots of reassurance and encouragement, and praise Hamish when he plays on large equipment

CASE STUDY 8

A child who shows no fear or is impulsive

Jack loves the big toys and the outdoors at pre-school. He constantly makes a beeline for the door and runs outside into the outdoor play area. He will climb on the equipment and jump off the top apparently oblivious to any danger. He has hurt himself on several occasions but this does not deter him. He is just so fast that it is difficult for the staff to keep track of where he is.

Possible reasons for this behaviour

Jack:
- has surplus energy and uses all opportunities for outdoor physical play. He may have limited space for this type of movement at home
- has hyperactivity difficulties and a very short attention span. He does not recognise the consequence of his actions
- has sensory integration difficulties
- may have learning difficulties or social communication difficulties

Strategies

- Use outdoor physical play as a reward for good behaviour. In this way, the outdoor play will be controlled by pre-school staff rather than by Jack. One suggestion would be that he is given a small laminated piece of card divided into four segments. He is told that whenever he does something good, one of the adult staff will put a smiley face on the chart. When he has four smiley faces he can go out to play for five minutes (as measured by a timer). Initially it will be very important that Jack's card is filled several times each session so that he becomes familiar with the process. Reward him for all the little things he does, such as a pleasant smile or walking nicely
- Monitor Jack's behaviour in other areas to determine if he has attention difficulties. It will be helpful to discuss this behaviour with his parents/carers
- Discuss Jack's behaviour with a medical professional. He may be affected by food additives
- Jack may not have been taught to consider the consequences of his actions. Devise a specific programme focusing on consequences. This could be done through pictures or story books
- Implement a structured system of activities which are rewarded with a time outdoors. This could be through a visual or concrete timetable such as showing Jack the puzzles and saying, 'First puzzle, then slide.' This will need to become established as a pattern for Jack so that he needs to carry out a specific very short activity before playing outdoors or on the big equipment. This type of system is likely to need adult support to become established and maintained

CASE STUDY 9

A child who avoids toys such as tricycles and scooters

Shannon will sit happily at a craft table in the book corner. She will play in the home corner and enjoys playdough. Shannon does not ever choose the sit-on toys and has never been seen to push teddy or dolly in the pushchair. Her mum says that Shannon still sits in a buggy when they go out.

Possible reasons for this behaviour

Shannon:
- finds these activities tiring. This may need medical investigation especially if Shannon has low energy in other areas
- has had a bad experience with a wheeled toy in the past and this has frightened her
- is frightened by the unpredictability of the children riding on these vehicles
- may have vision or hearing difficulties
- may have gross motor skill difficulties
- may have been involved in or witnessed a motoring accident

Strategies

- Encourage Shannon to sit on a tricycle without moving on it
- Allow Shannon to try out the vehicles when no other children are there
- Have an adult push Shannon around initially until she develops greater confidence
- Monitor Shannon's motor skills and discuss concerns with her parents. If necessary, her parents could ask for a motor skills assessment through their GP. Visual and hearing difficulties should also be eliminated
- Look at books about vehicles in a small group or individual situation. Shannon could be encouraged to talk about vehicles she has or knows about

CASE STUDY 10

A child who refuses to play an adult-led or organised game

Ben is very happy to play with the toys and equipment in the pre-school and is quite content to spend time with his friends enjoying the large wheeled apparatus. However, whenever an adult approaches him to ask if he will come to the table to join a game or task, he refuses or makes a half-hearted attempt and then leaves the group. This is presenting the staff with problems because they feel unable to assess his level of progress with the curriculum as he rarely joins them at the writing or maths table.

Possible reasons for this behaviour

Ben:

- is not ready to participate in formalised tasks. His behaviour may be a reflection of his general cognitive level
- is aware that tasks led by adults may be too difficult for him and rather than fail, he does not take part
- does not understand what is being asked of him
- is used to doing what he wants, when he wants
- finds the tasks are boring compared to the toys on offer in the pre-school
- has not reached the developmental level at which the tasks are pitched

Strategies

- Give Ben more time to play in an unstructured way and also to experience more physical forms of play before he is ready to take part in more formal styles of learning
- Instruct the adults around Ben to use less language while talking to him, so that he has more chance of understanding the key words and hence what is being asked of him
- Give Ben clear boundaries and expectations and reinforce these every day. He may need to have a better understanding of the expectations that adults in the pre-school have in the way of behaviour
- Make sure tasks reflect a broad and balanced curriculum and the experiences of the children. Writing and maths can just as easily be carried out outside in the play area and children who find sitting at tables difficult often respond more positively outdoors. If they are engaged in interesting activities outdoors they are more likely to want to think about basic concepts such as size, shape, colour, length etc. For example, if Ben can draw a snail and its shell on the outdoor chalk board and compare its length to that of other snails collected by the children, staff will have a pretty good idea of his general level of understanding in several areas of the curriculum
- Prepare an Individual Education Plan (IEP) for Ben in order to improve his ability to take part in adult-led activities (see Appendix 1)

CASE STUDY 11

A child who always plays 'mum' in the home corner

Victoria loves dressing up and playing in the home corner. She likes to choose the children who play with her and she always has to be the 'mum'. In fact, whenever she plays this she insists on being in charge and dominates the play. If another child attempts to exert any control, Victoria becomes upset and cannot accept the situation. She has, on occasion, used physical means like pushing the child away in order to make her feelings clear.

Possible reasons for this behaviour

Victoria:
- is enacting what she perceives her own mother is doing
- likes to have complete control over what she is doing and does not enjoy the uncertainty of not knowing what is going to happen
- has a dominant personality
- may be a very able child
- may be the eldest sibling in the family and is given a lot of responsibility at home
- may be the youngest in the family and is using the pre-school situation in order to redress the balance

Strategies

- Allow Victoria to experience short periods when someone else is 'mum'. She could choose the person so that she maintains some control. Encourage her to allow this other child to be 'mum' for a set period of time, e.g. until the sand timer has run out. Victoria could then be 'mum' again for the same short amount of time. She should be encouraged to say what she enjoyed about *not* being mum
- Encourage Victoria to play other games so that her play skills are extended
- Encourage Victoria to extend her circle of friends
- Make sure that Victoria's learning plan is challenging and that resources are stimulating
- Allow Victoria to use her leadership skills in other areas of learning, e.g. give her responsibilities which encourage and extend her interpersonal skills, or channel her natural instincts to be in charge by giving her the opportunity to help the adults with useful organisational tasks
- Talk to Victoria about letting other children be 'mum' and the reasons why this is a good idea

CASE STUDY 12

A child who refuses to let others play the same 'game' as them

Alzbeta likes to play with a particular pushchair and doll and she likes to play with this for most of the time. Not only does she like to have the same pushchair and doll but she also likes to push it on the same route around the play area. If another child attempts to join her game, Alzbeta becomes very upset, pushing the child away. Alzbeta refers to this particular pushchair and doll as 'my baby'.

Possible reasons for this behaviour

Alzbeta may:
- need 'props' in order to feel secure
- not have pushchairs or dolls to play with at home
- have very limited play skills
- not enjoy being away from home and her mother and this repetitive play is a source of comfort and security

Strategies

- Put the pushchairs away for part of the session
- Encourage Alzbeta to play alongside an adult who will model play skills with a variety of toys
- Observe Alzbeta playing with different toys, especially role-play equipment, and use these to target possible areas of need
- Pair Alzbeta up with a child who has excellent play skills and set up situations to encourage and extend Alzbeta's interest in other toys

CASE STUDY 13

A child who cannot accept losing a game (snakes and ladders)

Sean has to be seen to be winning at whatever he plays. This is especially obvious when playing more organised games such as lotto or snakes and ladders. If the game takes a slightly negative turn, e.g. if Sean's counter lands on a snake and he has to go down it, he will often end up by leaving the table and refusing to play on. However, while things are going in his favour, he is able to complete the game.

Possible reasons for this behaviour

Sean:
- is unable to deal with any perceived criticism or setback
- is used to having his own way
- sees even a slight setback in an exaggerated form
- has low self-esteem and is confusing setbacks with a personal slight
- has not had any real setbacks in his life and is shielded from anything negative
- does not fully understand the game

Strategies

- Explain and, if possible, demonstrate a game to the children before starting, using very simple language. Do not assume that children know or have understood how to play
- Explain that sometimes, you have to go backwards (or down the snake) and that you always have a chance to catch up and that other people will have setbacks too
- Use social stories and role play. This may help to get Sean used to the idea that sometimes negative things will happen and that there is always a way of dealing with them
- Pay attention to the way Sean behaves in other situations to see if this kind of behaviour is part of his generalised pattern. If it is so, Sean's self-esteem may be low. (See our first book *Behaviour in the Early Years* (Glenn *et al.* 2004).)
- Encourage Sean to separate things that he has control over from those that he does not

CASE STUDY 14

A child who cannot play by set rules

Andrew is happy to play with other children and has three boys with whom he particularly likes to play. As soon as the game becomes involved enough to warrant rules, e.g. 'You are not allowed to get me when I go behind this tree', Andrew seems to deliberately ignore the rules. Games almost always end in arguments. When an adult is setting out the rules of a table-top game, Andrew often ignores these, deliberately moving his counter in any way he sees fit. Although the adults end up barring Andrew from the games, he always makes a fuss about it.

Possible reasons for this behaviour

Andrew:
- is deliberately causing a 'drama' because he enjoys the attention
- likes to be in charge and resents it if others make up rules
- cannot understand the idea of rules and why we have them
- is not used to following rules set by others
- is used to getting his own way
- knows that if he 'holds out' for long enough, he will eventually get his own way

Strategies

- Explain why we have to have rules in order to play some games
- Encourage Andrew to make up some rules for games that other people have to stick to. His friends could do the same and Andrew has to stick to their rules
- Make the consequences of not playing or sticking to rules very clear
- Talk to Andrew about situations where we have to obey rules, e.g. at traffic lights, and what would happen if people did not obey them

CASE STUDY 15

A child who dislikes playing outside

Emma always chooses to play inside even though there is an 'open door' policy at her pre-school. If adults persuade her to go into the garden, she just stands around and eventually finds her way back inside. Sometimes the adults do not even notice her making her way in. Emma is a popular and lively child with a good sense of humour and no one can make sense of her constant choice of playing inside.

Possible reasons for this behaviour

Emma:
- is really interested in the toys and equipment in the indoor room
- doesn't feel secure outside
- finds some activities outside frightening
- cannot hear or see clearly what is going on outside
- may not have a garden at home and is used to being inside
- may associate being outdoors with a negative episode

Strategies

- Arrange to have Emma's eyesight and hearing checked
- Find out what is attractive to Emma about the indoor space and what is unappealing about the outdoor one. If there are activities or apparatus which are unfamiliar to her, adults should model their uses and encourage her to participate for minimal periods at first
- Regularly carry out Emma's favourite activities outside. She will learn to make positive associations with the outdoor area. Indeed, the whole session could be conducted outside as a matter of course

CASE STUDY 16

A child who always plays with one particular child

Jade only plays with one particular child at the pre-school. If that child is absent, Jade just sits by herself. She is co-operative with adults and joins in with tasks but will not play with any other child during the free play session. When her particular friend is at the pre-school, Jade dislikes being joined in a game by anyone else.

Possible reasons for this behaviour

Jade:
- is very insecure
- has been spurned by another child/other children and lacks confidence now in playing with others
- is trying to maintain some control over matters in the pre-school
- is not used to being with large groups of people
- is an only child
- comes from a very self-contained family and is content with having just one friend

Strategies

- Include Jade in small-group activities (just one other child at first) as a regular feature of the day and gradually increase the size of the groups
- Investigate Jade's interests and use these to include her in group work with other children
- Pair Jade with different children during the session so that she is exposed to a variety of characters. If Jade is happy to associate with just one child and all avenues have been explored, then it may be that this is part of her personality at the present time
- Investigate whether any of the other children live near to Jade's house to extend relationships outside the pre-school

CASE STUDY 17

A child whose play is repetitive

Amir likes to play with cars and trains whenever he gets the chance. He just pushes the cars back and forth and does the same with the trains although he uses the tracks sometimes. When Amir plays with balls he tends to bang them against the wall, appearing to enjoy the sound of the banging. Amir often chooses toys and balls that make a noise. Similarly, when Amir plays with the tricycles, he usually uses them to rock back and forth. In the home corner, Amir puts all the dishes into the dishwasher and then takes them all out. He often repeats the process. When adults or children try to talk to Amir, he ignores them and often looks in the opposite direction or down at the floor.

Possible reasons for this behaviour

Amir:
- does not have many toys at home
- lacks experiences especially of role play
- has autistic spectrum disorder (ASD)

Strategies

- Observe Amir closely and decide whether he just lacks experience or whether a paediatric assessment would help
- Model play skills and encourage Amir, using simple language focusing on key words as much as possible
- Use visual aids whenever possible to maximise Amir's understanding of language
- Make observations and assessments regarding Amir's understanding of language and basic concepts and consider a referral to a speech and language therapist who may be able to help clarify Amir's needs

CASE STUDY 18

A child who only engages in play if directed by an adult

Jenna is a quiet child who co-operates with adult requests and joins in with all the activities in the pre-school. However, it has been noticed that she does this after direction from an adult and hardly ever acts spontaneously. This feature of her behaviour is even more obvious when she is in the outdoor area and during the sessions of free play. Adults invariably find her standing alone and just observing the other children. When she is approached and a suggestion is made about playing with a particular toy, she complies with the suggestion and plays appropriately.

Possible reasons for this behaviour

Jenna:
- is a very quiet child who prefers to observe rather than join in
- dislikes being in the pre-school but has been brought up to be compliant with adults
- finds the activities boring and fails to see the point of them
- lacks confidence and feels it is safer to wait until asked to do something in case she makes a mistake
- is used to having to wait until told to do something and may think this is the correct way to behave

Strategies

- Gently encourage Jenna to realise that when she feels ready, then she is at liberty to choose from any of the activities on offer. If it is thought that Jenna is a quiet child and likes to observe others she should be allowed to do this as part of her natural personality
- Have a trusted adult make gentle enquiries about whether Jenna likes coming to the pre-school and about what her personal interests are. If Jenna can tell the adults what she likes doing, perhaps these things can be included into the sessions so that Jenna feels that her views are important and that she has something to look forward to doing
- Be aware of her cognitive development and consider whether she is being challenged

CASE STUDY 19

A child who always seeks out (holds the hand of) an adult during outside play sessions

Toni always attaches herself to an adult by holding their hand when she is outside and will attempt to stay with that person for the entire session. When other children approach her and ask her to join them she becomes even more attached to the adult, holding on to their hand more tightly. All suggestions and encouragements from staff fail to engage Toni in the activities on offer.

Possible reasons for this behaviour

Toni:
- is frightened of the apparatus on offer outside which seems (to her) to be very different from things on offer indoors
- has a hearing or visual problem
- lacks confidence with the more physical apparatus
- lacks experience of the outdoors – does she live in an apartment without access to a garden?
- has been told that she must stay with an adult whenever she is outdoors
- is seeking attention – perhaps in response to a new baby at home?

Strategies

- Be aware of differences between the use of outdoor and indoor areas. Activities which are carried out indoors should be interchangeable with activities outdoors. For example, drawing doesn't need only to be done inside, it can easily be transported to the outdoor areas. Similarly, using the climbing frame can be an indoor activity. If Toni likes table-top activities these should be on offer outdoors
- Gradually encourage Toni to play with the larger wheeled toys and apparatus so that staff can make assessments about her gross motor skills and balance. This should be done with adult support at first
- Ask Toni's parents or carers whether her hearing and vision have been checked. If her hearing and vision are normal, staff should encourage her to widen her use of apparatus by introducing them one at a time and emphasising how much fun they can be. Adults should model how to use the apparatus
- Pair Toni up with a 'buddy' who could play with her on something she doesn't normally use, e.g. a two-seater tricycle
- If there is a new baby at home encourage Toni to talk about her brother/sister and praise her for helping Mummy etc.

CASE STUDY 20

A child who becomes upset when faced with unfamiliar situations

Anthony is four and a half years old and is very content to play and to participate with tasks in the pre-school and seems to enjoy all the activities on offer. However, if the session has some changes to it or if there is an unfamiliar adult in the room, Anthony starts to cry. It always takes him some time to calm down and a high level of adult support is needed to bring this about. When Anthony stops crying, he carries on as normal but frequently approaches a known adult for reassurance. Anthony has behaved like this for a long time and adults have become so used to it that they now expect it and think nothing of it. Anthony's mother still phones the setting regularly to enquire about his behaviour.

Possible reasons for this behaviour

Anthony:
- has learned that crying results in some individual attention
- is genuinely upset when something unexpected happens and is linking this to an earlier trauma
- is picking up his mother's possible anxieties

Strategies

- Organise a discussion with Anthony's mother. This may provide a clearer idea of what is behind his behaviour
- Consider the possibility that child protection may be an issue
- Warn Anthony when it is known that there will be a visitor or when something different is going to happen
- Continue to support Anthony when he becomes distressed but spend less and less time with him. The adults could gradually withdraw their support and expect that he will learn to cope with minimal adult intervention. It should be emphasised how well Anthony is doing by himself and even reward him when he shows signs of coping without adults
- Use stories about visits and surprises in order to highlight the positive, fun aspects of unexpected events happening

CASE STUDY 21

A child who always plays with 'baby' toys

Samantha is four years old and loves to play with the younger children in the pre-school and almost always chooses activities and toys associated with very young children or even babies. Whenever there is a free play session she will invariably choose from the box containing things like stacking toys and shape posting boxes. Sometimes Samantha will deliberately choose the starter puzzles with four or five pieces and do these over and over again. The staff are not concerned about Samantha's progress in other areas.

Possible reasons for this behaviour

Samantha:
- lacks the confidence to try new activities
- finds security in knowing that she will be able to carry out tasks easily
- may not have made friends with children of her own age
- may have a new baby brother/sister and she is playing with the toys that remind her of home
- may not have had a large variety of toys when she was very young and is discovering them for the first time
- may have a real fear of failure and chooses things she knows she will be able to do successfully

Strategies

- Carry out focused observations about the kind of things Samantha is choosing, who she interacts with and how
- Let a 'buddy' help Samantha integrate with her own peer group
- Encourage Samantha to engage in more age-appropriate activities in small focused groups at first. This could be started by using a toy/equipment that is related to her favourite activity but which is more appropriate to her ability level
- Staff should highlight the things Samantha is good at if she is lacking in confidence and give her some responsibilities in the pre-school
- Let Samantha know that it is OK to fail – that everyone (including adults) makes mistakes or that when we do something for the first time it feels awkward and it may not work out instantly but that it is the same for everyone. She may need to observe this directly herself and staff may have to contrive some situations in which they 'make mistakes' and react in a level-headed manner. She may need to see people trying the same activity repeatedly in order to achieve results
- Talk to Samantha's parents/carers to ask about her play preferences at home

CASE STUDY 22

A child who becomes out of control and overexcited during boisterous activity

Harry is a popular boy who loves to be involved in all activities in the pre-school. He is a polite, well-behaved child who follows instructions and is confident. However, whenever there is a more physical or boisterous activity going on, Harry becomes quite out of control, very excited and appears not to be able to hear adults giving him instructions about expected behaviour. This happens especially when there is an outdoor activity which involves a lot of physical activity. Harry's dad often brings him to and collects him from the pre-school. It has been noted that as soon as Harry sees his dad, he throws himself at him and they begin a 'wrestling match'.

Possible reasons for this behaviour

Harry:
- associates active sessions with a kind of 'free for all' with very few restrictions on behaviour
- sees active sessions as a time for 'letting off steam'
- may have a surplus of energy and gets rid of it during physical activity
- may have a high blood sugar level
- associates 'rough and tumble' games with a high 'fun factor'

Strategies

- Be very clear about the rules of behaviour when engaging in physical activity and outline these *before* the activity begins. Ideally the rules should be in picture form. Harry may need a personalised 'rule book'
- Explain that although some people like rough games, not everyone does and that some people find it frightening. Also, some people do not like to be tugged, pulled etc.
- Make sure that activities carried out outdoors span the entire curriculum and should not be confined to the more physical activities. In this way, children will not associate the outdoor area with a limited choice of activities
- Discuss Harry's behaviour with his parents to see if Harry is the same at home. If they have the same problem there, a consistent plan of action will help
- Take Harry outside regularly for quiet activities
- Make sure that Harry gets regular outdoor, physical exercise and check with his parents that he is eating a balanced diet

CASE STUDY 23

A child who cannot wait for his/her turn

Milos is very keen to participate in everything on offer at the pre-school. So keen, in fact, that he is bursting to answer questions in whole-group sessions, often blurting out answers before the adult has finished talking. During games, Milos has difficulty waiting for his turn and just takes his turn before anyone can intervene. Milos acts on impulse and doesn't seem to think first. When engaging in physical activities, Milos can behave very dangerously, throwing himself from the climbing frame without warning. When his attention is drawn to this, Milos appears not to know what he has done wrong.

Possible reasons for this behaviour

Milos may:
- be a very energetic individual who just needs to direct his energy more effectively
- not understand the social rules of behaviour, e.g. turn taking and being aware that other people have feelings which need to be taken account of
- have a poor sense of the consequences of his own actions
- be affected by ADHD (attention deficit hyperactivity disorder)

Strategies

- List the behaviours which are causing concern
- Be aware of the health and safety issues connected with Milos's impulsive behaviour
- Refer Milos to a paediatrician in order to eliminate possible medical reasons for his behaviour
- Implement very good behaviour management planning. Milos may require a behaviour plan so that staff are consistent in managing him
- Let Milos know exactly what the expectations are *before* the activity begins
- Reward Milos whenever he demonstrates wanted behaviours
- Ensure that a high degree of structure and a visually strong method of teaching are used for Milos's benefit
- Discuss the consequences of different types of behaviour so that Milos begins to develop an awareness of his own actions. Using puppets and social stories might be two ways of dealing with this
- Prepare an IEP for Milos in order to improve his ability to take turns (see Appendix 1)

CASE STUDY 24

A child who cannot adapt to the suggestions of others during games or activities

Lucy simply refuses to carry on with games if other children make suggestions which do not match her own. If Lucy's rules are not adhered to, she finds it impossible to carry on with the game. Lucy often ends up in tears of frustration when she cannot get her own way and takes some time to recover her composure. Lucy has great difficulty accepting that she cannot always be first in line or the one who has done the 'best' painting.

Possible reasons for this behaviour

Lucy:
- is used to being in control of situations
- has been told that she is better at things than other children
- may be an only child or the youngest child in the family and is being indulged because of this
- has worked out that when she insists on things or cries, it results in her getting her own way

Strategies

- Give Lucy realistic assessments of her achievements. Her strengths should be highlighted
- Help Lucy to see that listening to others is a positive thing and that other people have valuable things to say. Social stories may help or using whole-group times in order to discuss this issue in an anonymous manner. To find out more about social stories contact your pre-school advisory services. The library have a range of books dealing with specific subject areas
- Give Lucy some control over situations. She could be allowed to choose a friend to join a group playing a simple game. The decision as to who should 'go' first could be shared by the group so that all the children have the chance to 'be in charge'. In this way (where there are set rules) Lucy will be able to see the advantages of working co-operatively. At first, an adult should supervise and prompt the children if necessary, but the adult should gradually withdraw so that the children can act independently

CASE STUDY 25

A child who uses a lot of violence in play

Billy is very much a loner in the pre-school and usually plays by himself. He sometimes attempts to engage with the other children but joins their activities without being asked and more or less imposes himself upon them. He likes to play with the dolls' house or in the home corner. The staff have observed that he uses the dolls to re-enact scenes that look quite violent. The dolls throw things around the house and tip the furniture up. Billy keeps a running commentary going while he plays and uses shouting to re-enact confrontations between the dolls. Billy plays this game most days at the pre-school and when staff attempt to talk to him he responds minimally and then goes off to play with something else. When Billy plays with the dolls in the home corner, he has been observed being very rough with them and 'smacking' them regularly.

Possible reasons for this behaviour

Billy:
- watches a lot of television and is reproducing what he sees
- has quite limited play skills and repeats the same game because of this. It may reflect a general cognitive delay
- may be copying behaviour modelled by adults he lives with
- may be trying to make sense of what he has seen by re-enacting it in the dolls' house

Strategies

- Monitor Billy's activities very closely and note these down factually
- There could be child protection issues – ensure staff are aware of procedures
- Make sure that Billy engages in a wide range of activities if staff believe him to have limited play skills. Resources should be planned with care to take account of this
- Monitor Billy's general progress with the curriculum closely
- Discuss the issues with Billy's parents/carers

SECTION 3

Play skills

- Developing play skills

- Developing imaginative play

- Positive Play – a programme for children with poor social skills

Developing play skills

Children need to develop a range of skills in order to utilise play experiences to the full. These can be considered in six areas and generally, there needs to be a fairly balanced development in each one. The six areas are:

- **Social** – where the child shows an interest in other people and begins to develop empathy

- **Communication** – where the child wants to communicate through verbal and non-verbal communication

- **Fine motor skills** – where the child develops fine motor co-ordination and dexterity

- **Gross motor skills** – which are related to mobility and body posture

- **Imagination and thinking skills** – needed for pretend play

- **Attention** – where the child develops concentration and focused attention

It can be very useful to use the following tables as a checklist to consider children's strengths and the areas in which they may need support at different ages and stages.

Developmental stages for social and communication skills		
Approx. age	**Social skills**	**Communication skills**
0–6 months	Child develops feelings of security and trust if given consistent approaches.	Child enjoys watching faces and will initiate expressions. Enjoys soothing calm sounds.
6–18 months	Child begins to recognise him or herself as a separate person. Begins to recognise that certain actions produce an effect. Enjoys repetitive rhymes and anticipating actions.	Child begins to babble. Will imitate sounds and gestures. Will often practise sounds on their own.
18 months–3 years	Parallel play. Will play alongside other children. Can initiate play with adults by bringing a toy to an adult. Can be led into activities by an adult and will join in.	Joins in with rhymes and action songs. Enjoys repetition of stories. Can name pictures and make sounds in imitation, e.g. animals. Can talk about actions.
3–4 years	Joins in with groups. Initiates contact with other children and plays with others.	Knows words of songs and rhymes and can sing unaided. Can talk about an object or event without it being there.
4–5 years	Co-operative play – can play by rules and can design own rules.	Reciprocal communication and conversations. Takes turns in conversation.

Developmental stages for fine motor and gross motor skills

Approx. age	Fine motor skills	Gross motor skills
0–6 months	Turns head and hands to music or movement. Enjoys rattles and mobiles.	Develops head control. Turns head in direction of sound or movement. Can sit propped up.
6–18 months	Explores using mouth. Interested in and explores environment. Makes sounds by banging objects.	Can sit unaided. Can stand and cruise round furniture. Has independent mobility.
18 months–3 years	Can play peek-a-boo. Enjoys cause and effect toys. Beginning to match objects and to sort objects. Enjoys sand and water play.	Prefers to play outdoors or on floor. Benefits by a supportive chair with arms near a table to become involved in mealtimes, or an activity. Bean bags can be helpful.
3–4 years	Enjoys creative aspects, e.g. cooking, playdough, sticking. Can do jigsaws.	Active play – enjoys climbing frame and apparatus and sit-on/push-along/pedal toys. If trying to encourage group circle time activities, a bean bag can be useful for support.
4–5 years	Can build with a range of construction equipment which involves good fine motor skills.	Enjoys floor activities. Works best with a supportive chair with back for table-top activities.

Developmental stages for skills of pretend play and attention to task

Approx. age	Pretend play	Attention to task
0–6 months	Responds to sound and movement in view.	Responds to any new sound or movement stimulation.
6–18 months	Initiates actions of others. Repeats this on own, e.g. feeding teddy.	Prefers own choice of activity and can become very involved. There can be a difficulty in following an adult-led activity.
18 months–3 years	Uses teddy and dolly to perform actions. 'Pretend' objects are evident in play, e.g. make-up and cup of tea to drink using toy cup.	Able to follow adult-led activity. Needs adult to sustain concentration. Focuses on one area at a time and can become highly involved. Switching attention needs adult direction.
3–4 years	Can use toys and objects to act out recent events. Becomes very involved in make-believe play such as home corner, shopping etc.	Becoming less easily distracted from adult-led tasks. Can switch attention from one activity to another. Needs to stop activity to listen to instructions.
4–5 years	Uses own imagination for role play, e.g. fairies, dragons etc.	Can carry out a task and listen to instructions at the same time.

Developing imaginative play

This is an area that warrants close observation as it can give us good quality information about a child. At the early stage of play, children will imitate the actions of others, particularly if they are encouraged to do so. Following this stage, there are two main stages involved:

Stage 1 in which the child uses real objects as representations and props. This is a concrete level of play and can involve solitary or shared experiences. Examples are:

- feeding a dolly or teddy using a pretend bottle
- making dinner using plastic plates and food
- pushing teddy in a pushchair
- pretending to write out a shopping list using pencil and paper
- pushing toy cars around a track

Stage 2 in which a more abstract level of play develops. There are two types of examples:

1. The child enters imaginary situations without any props, such as:
   - making a cup of tea using only actions
   - pretending to be in a car and driving
   - making and eating an imaginary cake
   - running away from an imaginary dragon or other creature
   - opening a door and going inside using actions

2. The child gives objects or people other functions, such as:
   - a teddy, doll or another child becomes the baby or parent
   - playing at shops being a shopkeeper and customer
   - playing hospitals and being doctors and nurses
   - being a fireman, police officer or angel in the dressing-up corner
   - using puppets or toys to become other characters

Most children will go naturally through these stages whereas others will need support in developing Stage 2 play. If a child appears stuck at Stage 1 they may need to have Stage 2 activities demonstrated to them so that they can initially copy them and join in games. It will also be important to notice whether the child at Stage 1 is mainly or solely engaged in solitary play or whether they are able to join in shared activities.

A close observation of pretend play can yield some very interesting information. Some children look totally absorbed in their activity but on closer observation they are simply lining up cars or trains or are filling and emptying the washing machine in the home corner. This observation is particularly important to use as information for children who are likely to have difficulties in social communication areas or may be having emotional difficulties. Some of these children may not be ready to engage in some of the activities and although they can be encouraged to imitate, they may not be able to use these skills on their own. Further advice may be needed from the area Special Educational Needs Co-ordinator (SENCO) or educational psychologist on how best to support the child.

Positive Play – a programme for children with poor social skills

The majority of children settle happily into the early years setting – some take a bit longer than others and may go through a shy or tearful phase while others bounce into the room with confidence from day one. A lot depends on their experiences prior to joining your nursery or playschool. If they have already experienced playing with other children, have visited other people's houses, been to the park and discovered the excitement and pitfalls of swings and slides and have learnt how to cope with sharing toys and games with brothers and sisters they will probably cope with most early years situations.

However, from time to time a child enrols with your nursery/playgroup and just does not seem to be able to pick up the rules and routines in the usual way. Sometimes children become withdrawn or tearful and need a lot of cajoling and persuading to join in. They can be reluctant to even enter the room or venture out into the outdoor area. These children need sensitive handling and to be allowed time just to sit and watch what is going on. More often than not these shy children are able to overcome their reservations if given the opportunity.

Other individuals can behave in an overly boisterous or even aggressive manner, snatching toys and throwing sand, shouting and pushing others away from 'their' space and refusing all efforts to distract them from causing upset all round. This can be a major problem in the outdoor area where it is often more difficult for the adults to monitor closely all that is going on. Children may find the outdoors difficult for a variety of reasons including lack of experience, finding the range of activities on offer overwhelming, having problems understanding what is expected of them or perhaps having difficulties associated with autistic spectrum disorder (ASD). Whatever the cause, if this sort of behaviour continues, and particularly if the time for moving on to mainstream school is imminent, then it may well be useful to have a planned programme of intervention to address the problem. A detailed, time-limited programme of activities, targeting specific skills and carried out on a daily or weekly basis for a set number of weeks, can help the child develop the necessary skills to have a successful and enjoyable time. Such a programme will also provide valuable information of the child's needs which can be passed on to the school. Positive Play is our own tried and tested programme.

Setting up the programme

When working with very young children who are experiencing difficulties a 'little and often' approach is usually the best. It is also essential that *all* those involved with the child are fully included in the programme and this starts with meeting with the parents/carers to get them on board with the programme. A friendly but businesslike meeting should be set up to explain to the family your concerns about the child's needs and to discuss the intervention you are proposing. They should be invited to offer ideas for supporting the programme at home. These interviews can be difficult as many parents will be just hoping that their child will grow out of the snatching and pushing phase. It is therefore important that the parents/carers have been kept fully aware of their child's progress right from the start of their attendance in your setting so that it does not come as too much of a surprise to them that their child needs extra support. If it is felt appropriate the parents can be provided with a simple star chart to stick on the fridge at home to encourage good, co-operative behaviour at home too. At this initial meeting it is important to set a date to review the child's progress at the end of the six-week programme. Hopefully the child will have made considerable improvement during half a term but this review meeting can be used to discuss any further input which may be necessary.

It will help when setting up the programme if a formal observation of the child has been carried out using an observation chart similar to the one in Appendix 1. These observations, taken for about ten or 15 minutes at a time during different parts of the session, can really help to show up when the problems are occurring. It will also help to identify any other children who could benefit from being included in the programme or those who could be included as good role models.

An experienced member of staff needs to be identified as the main deliverer, or key adult, of the programme. This person will need to be released for at least 45 minutes each week for the whole six weeks of the programme to be responsible for running the programme and providing continuity and daily follow-up. Very often a child will behave very well in the structured 45-minute session but find it difficult to sustain turn taking or speaking kindly at other times of the week. It is important that all the staff know what is being implemented so that they can also be in a position to reinforce the programme at other times of the day. It will seriously undermine the success of the programme if, for instance, the week's target is focusing on sharing toys but inadvertently a member of staff totally ignores some snatching and pushing without using a rule reminder that 'we share toys'.

Typical targets for addressing behaviours during the programme may well include:
- allowing another child to play alongside (without pushing)
- playing safely in the outside area
- taking turns with e.g. a spade (with an adult)
- taking turns with equipment (with another child)
- returning indoors when asked

- using indoor/outdoor voice appropriately
- sitting quietly during snack time
- allowing others to listen to a story (without calling out)

When setting targets it is important that they are as specific as possible. Playing 'nicely' is far too vague to be measurable. Sharing a toy for a set period of time (anything from one minute at a time up to, say, ten minutes) will be far more useful as evidence of a child's progress. Simple notes will need to be kept of progress and will provide evidence of what parts of the programme have been least and most successful. Every child is an individual but following a core set of activities during the programme will make it easier to deliver similar interventions to others in the future.

Once the parent interview, staff briefing and target setting have been done the programme itself can be started. All early years settings are different but a sample plan is outlined below.

A sample programme

Week One

Each session the key adult takes the child by the hand and leads him or her to the selected activity area in the room, gathering up the two or three others who are going to share the activity and at the same time explaining that 'we play safely' in our pre-school and telling the child what is going to happen next, e.g. 'Today we are going to play with the sand with Jo and Annie.' Explain clearly the expected behaviour: 'I want you to play safely and keep the sand in the sand tray – then you can move on to your favourite activity . . .'. By having a pre-arranged set of activities which have been shared with the parents and all the other adults involved, it is possible for everyone to discuss with the child at the start of the day what is going to be happening. A large timer can be very useful to assist in keeping the child focused (e.g. '*When* the sand has all gone through, *then* we can go to the next activity.').

Once the child has played safely for the set number of minutes (and this can vary from individual to individual – some may be unable to manage more than about two minutes at a time), they should be invited to take the adult's hand and walk sensibly to the next activity. Some children will benefit by being taken by the hand for a walk round the outdoor area as the adult points out examples of happy, co-operative play, e.g. 'Look at John and Ahmed – they are having a good time sharing the scooter properly so each has a turn.'

It is important that each section of the programme follows a similar pattern so that a routine is established right from the start:

1. Rule reminder before the activity (e.g. we play safely and never hurt others)
2. Short activity with the key adult and two or three other children, while encouraging discussion about playing safely and using praise effectively: 'I really like the way you are waiting for Annie to fill her bucket. . .'
3. If necessary, a walk round the area and discussion about the activity while pointing out good behaviour of others

4. A second activity in which it will be necessary to share equipment and wait for a turn. It is often a good idea to contrive to make sure that there are not enough items for each child to have exclusive use of equipment so that they can practise asking for, and providing others with, fair shares

5. A final song or finger rhyme to end the session

6. Return to the main activity area

> Early years settings vary considerably but all will have a natural break or snack time of some kind. It will be helpful for the key worker to sit with the child and talk about the 'rules' for break time too.

Week Two

During the second week of the programme the key adult may wish to introduce another child to the programme to play alongside the target pupil, making sure that they know each other's name. Children who have displayed difficulty in playing co-operatively with others often appear to have a problem learning other children's names and it may help to develop their social skills if they are encouraged to address their peers by name (rather than just grabbing them!). Although the aim of the week is to encourage the children to play and talk co-operatively alongside each other, at the start of the week the adult needs to remain close by or in between them to forestall any argument or upsets. The format of the programme in Week Two remains similar to the first one, using whichever activities are on offer that week. With more children playing together the amount of conversation and use of vocabulary may well increase but the adult needs to ensure that the words 'fair', 'share', 'kind', 'turn', 'safe' etc. feature prominently. In the early years setting four children in the group is probably ideal but, depending on the social skills levels of the children, it may be possible to have six children working alongside each other.

Week Three

If all the children got on well in the second week and all seemed to benefit from playing together, it may be a good idea to keep the same grouping for the rest of the programme. On the other hand, if the adult feels that introducing a different child, either as well as or instead of the original friends, would be a good idea then this would be an ideal opportunity to do so.

By the end of Week Three it will probably become apparent if this input is having any effect. A short, formal observation using the same chart as before may be helpful to see if there are any pockets of major improvement or a noticeable lack of it. If there has been real improvement, then moving on to the second half of the programme can go ahead. However, if it appears that the child is still having major difficulties even socialising with one other child, then all the adults involved need to discuss the next best way forward. Having an adult working closely alongside the child may also have identified other difficulties that some children may be experiencing. Problems with naming colours, having poor hand–eye co-ordination or experiencing difficulties with expressive or receptive language may become apparent. Repeating Weeks One, Two and Three may well be the most feasible way of continuing the programme.

However, for the majority of children who respond well to this sort of programme it is normal to work on through the next three weeks of daily intervention.

Week Four

Sometimes it is not possible to keep the same member of staff working on the programme every week and if different personnel have to deployed on running the programme this can help to give valuable insight into a child's adaptability to change. During Week Four a *planned* change of key adult can be included in the programme and notes made on the child's ability to handle this change.

The fourth week should be the time for the adult to slightly step away from being part of the group and allow the children to generate their own conversations, providing the adult with an opportunity to do some observations and see how the social interactions are developing. The adult will need to be close enough, however, to step in and remind the children of rules, keep them on task, and defuse any potential upsetting or hurtful turns of conversation. Frequently used words should still be 'safe', 'share', 'turn', 'friend', 'kind' etc. When choosing the activities the adult needs to make sure that, for some of the time at least, there are not enough play items to go around so that the children need to come to an agreement on how to divide things up between themselves without the adult necessarily doing it for them. The skill of negotiating and the concept of fairness will be essential when they move into mainstream school where there are fewer adults on hand to 'sort things out'. This is not easy for many children and the adult may want to discuss the possibility of 'What would happen if . . .?' before going out into the outside area. The large size sand timer can be very useful when discussing 'fairness' and 'turns'.

The basic formula of the programme in Week Four remains the same but includes more ambitious activities such as making a cake or icing biscuits to be shared with others in the pre-school. Even tasks such as organising the drink and biscuits for the whole pre-school or helping to clear away may be undertaken, closely supervised by the key adult.

Week Five

In Week Five, if the children are co-operating well and have responded to the emphasis on turn taking and listening to others the adult may wish to introduce slightly more complicated or competitive games. For instance giant-sized snakes and ladders or an activity such as 'Friends and family circle' (see p. 50) can generate a lot of discussion and information sharing. Children who

Friends and family circle – explanation

The adult asks the children to draw a picture of themselves in the middle circle and the people closest to them (i.e. those who live with them) in the second circle. In the third circle the children draw people they see most days (these could be neighbours, relatives, pre-school friends and staff etc.). The children draw people they sometimes see in the next circle (e.g. doctors, shop-keepers, the postman). A final outer circle could be added for the children to draw people who they rarely see (e.g. relatives living abroad). Children who find drawing too challenging can be provided with a jar of buttons to represent themselves, their family and their friends.

See Appendix 2 for a blank template.

This activity can generate a lot of discussion and information sharing.

Friends and family circle – example

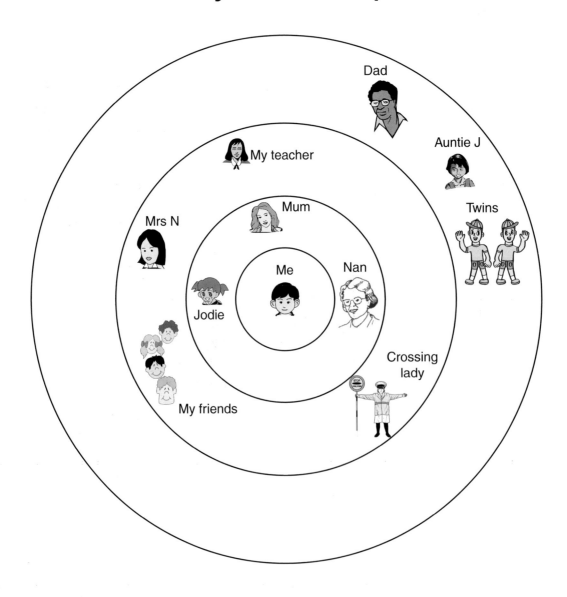

Children who find drawing difficult (e.g. those with fine motor difficulties who cannot hold a crayon or pencil) may prefer to use the box of buttons to aid completion of the circles. It may be interesting to observe which buttons are used for different people. Using the 'Teddy bear climbing frame' activity is another way of encouraging the children to share opinions and listen to others (see p. 52). Even if some of the children appear to be using the activity as 'just colouring the teddies', the skills of sharing the crayons, letting others have their say, and commenting on their own experiences of climbing frames are important so the adult need not necessarily feel the need to ask probing questions or insist on children expressing an opinion.

During Week Five it is important that the adult prepares the group for the next and last session. Each child is asked to choose another child from the pre-school and invite them to join their group for a drink and biscuits or fruit during Week Six. Many children no longer 'entertain' at home and have little experience of invitation and acceptances. In the pre-school this may be done by getting the children to actually send an invitation card to their chosen friend. They need to be encouraged to think carefully about whom they are going to invite – it may be a child who is new to the setting and needs to be helped to settle in, it may be someone who often does not have anyone to play with, or it may be someone that they have played with many times. It is also useful if the adult also invites another adult to join them for refreshments. If it is appropriate the parents/carers of the children in the group could be asked to send in a contribution, such as a packet of biscuits, some fruit etc.

Week Six

In Week Six the first activity should be the children sorting themselves out and arranging the refreshments attractively and making sure there are enough seats, cups and plates. Some plain paper to colour and make placemats is a useful way of keeping all the group occupied and gives the adult a chance to explain that they are going to look after their guest and make sure they have a drink and something to eat. The guest need not stay long as it is not necessary for the occasion to turn into a full-scale party. The children just need to practise their politeness, sharing and listening skills. It is also important that the children tidy up afterwards.

It is also useful for the adult to feed back to the parents any successes and progress that their child has made during the programme and give them an opportunity to feed back any improvements in their child's social skills that they have noticed at home. Keeping notes of strategies or games that have been particularly successful in developing social skills will be helpful if the pre-school decides to run a rolling programme of such interventions in the future and the comments of parents can aid the evaluation of this small-group work.

Teddy bear climbing activity – explanation

This is an activity to encourage discussion about feelings and to practise listening to others. This can be conducted as a one-to-one session with a child, or with a small group of children.

Materials needed:

- A copy of the teddy bear climbing frame picture for each member of the group, including the adult(s) (see Appendix 3)
- Coloured crayons or pencils

Ask everyone to look carefully at the teddy bears and see what they are doing. Encourage the children to say whether the teddies look happy, sad, worried, lonely, naughty etc. Invite the children to offer explanations of why they think a particular bear is feeling the way it is looking.

Ask the children to choose a crayon and colour in the bear they would like to be, allowing the children to talk about their choice. Then ask them to choose a different colour crayon and colour in the bear that they would not like to be or the one they feel sorry for.

Invite discussion as not all the children will choose the same bear and allow the conversation to flow with the emphasis on listening to others and taking turns to talk. If time allows, let the children finish colouring the whole picture and put them on display for others to look at.

SECTION 4

Top tips for creating a challenging play environment

Planning play

Six things to do every time when planning and teaching

Organising play

Managing staff

Using outdoor resources

Organising equipment for outdoor play

Observing behaviour

This section sets out in brief format some ideas you might like to think about when planning a challenging play and learning environment. The way in which you organise this is key to children's learning and development. Some questions you may ask are as follows.

How can I:
- support and extend learning though planning play activities?
- help children to be spontaneous?
- extend children's language and communication through play?
- help children make sense of the world around them?
- make children aware of the risks and challenges that (especially the outside) world presents?
- make sure that children experience things in a safe situation?

Obviously there will be restrictions upon some settings with regard to accessing an outdoor space. Even so, there are some suggestions below that may be useful if you want to bring some of the outdoors, indoors. Play in the Foundation Stage is the most important factor when planning the curriculum and all of it can be taught outdoors!

Top tips for planning play

- Make sure that planned activities have some connection to children's experiences
- When planning activities to build concepts like size, shape, height, weight consider teaching outdoors as much as possible
- Make these activities as much fun as possible, e.g. find the longest worm, the largest snail, the heaviest stone, the deepest puddle
- When planning creative activities consider using nature's designs, e.g. leaves, petals, spider's webs, shells, feathers
- When planning with your staff – make sure that *all* staff are enthusiastic about working outdoors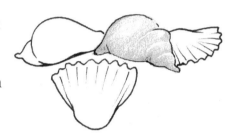
- Use visible rules outdoors so that children know what is expected of them
- Have a pictorial timetable (weatherproofed with laminate) on display
- Plan different areas and divide up indoor and outdoor spaces, e.g. outdoor quiet areas, running and throwing areas, digging areas, construction areas, sensory areas, creative areas, role-play areas
- Plan activities that are interchangeable between the indoor and outdoor environment so that children don't make a conscious distinction between 'learning takes place indoors with an adult present' and 'play takes place outside with my friends'

Six things to do every time when planning and teaching

- Identify teaching objectives and share these with the children
- Specify the exact behaviour expected
- Give clear instructions
- Specify the criteria for success
- Use rewards – praise
- Outline what support you will use, e.g. demonstrating the activity first so the children understand what to expect, use of physical prompts

Top tips for organising play

- Restrictions such as health and safety considerations and space available will have an impact, but consider creating a planting area indoors
- Have window boxes
- Snails and worms can be kept successfully indoors if there is no outdoor space
- Grow plants (flowers and vegetables) on sunny windowsills
- Hang rain gauges from hooks near windows
- Hang bird feeders near to the window
- Stick windmills on window frames
- Ask parents to donate wet weather clothing
- Place hooks for hanging outdoor clothing at child height near to the exit so that children can help themselves
- Keep small items such as magnifiers handy and in a place accessible to children
- Invest in large plastic boxes with lids for storage of equipment inside and out – label them with a picture and a word
- Link the indoor and outdoor area with a covered area and organise as one learning environment
- Use the outdoor area as a matter of course for story time, whole-group time, painting, counting, writing etc.

Top tips for managing staff

- Make sure that all staff are enthusiastic and are encouraged to work outside
- Staff need to be briefed and be clear about the reason for carrying out activities (is the aim of the task counting/caring for the environment etc.?)
- Staff require very specific teaching aims and objectives and need to share these with the children
- Staff should be role models for language/behaviours/interaction skills
- Children should be expected to do their own work (how many Mother's Day cards are made by the adults?)
- Staff should encourage children to be independent
- Staff require regular training and updating, including health and safety
- New and volunteer staff should receive some induction training including a sheet setting out all the expected modes of conduct

Top tips for using outdoor resources

- Use large stones or tree stumps as natural climbing blocks, tree trunks/branches for seats (check safety), pebbles, assortments of rock, small pieces of wood and shells to encourage exploration of natural materials
- Set up water and sand play areas outside where any mess created can be easily cleaned
- Encourage the children to care for plants by growing annual flowers (e.g. nasturtium), vegetables (e.g. lettuce, radish) and herbs (e.g. chives). The children can harvest and eat the salad crops. If space is limited these can be planted in tubs or window boxes. In autumn plant bulbs so the children can see them flower in spring
- Have indoor plants in pots on windowsills and encourage the children to take turns in watering them
- Grow plants in the outdoor space to attract birds and insects, e.g. buddleia to attract butterflies. The children can use magnifiers to study small insects
- Hang bird feeders on trees and hooks and have a bird bath to encourage garden birds to visit the outdoor area. Ask the children to help fill the feeders and in cold weather check that the bird bath is not iced over
- Create a small pond and stock it with fish (ensure it is covered with a safety net to prevent children from falling into it)
- Collect building and construction materials such as cardboard boxes, pieces of wood etc. These can be used for imaginative role-play games

Top tips for organising equipment for outdoor play

- Have a collection of wet weather clothing and footwear in case of drizzle or wet ground during outdoor play. A collection of extra clothing is also useful if the weather is unexpectedly cold
- Construct a Wendy house, shed or tents so the children can use these as a focus for role-play activities
- Encourage an awareness of the weather by having kites, windmills and streamers available for windy days and rain gauges to catch rain
- Collect gardening equipment, e.g. small watering cans and trowels that are suitable for small hands to cope with
- Encourage physical activity outside by having skipping ropes, balls (sponge and plastic), bats and skittles, tunnels to crawl through, wheeled toys, a rocking horse etc.
- For large-scale painting activities have a selection of large brushes (household-decorating size) available and materials to paint on, e.g. sheets of cardboard, old linen, walls
- Create a puppet theatre
- Make an outdoor chalk board
- Collect *real* pots and pans, kettles and telephones for the home corner

Top tips for observing behaviour

One of the most effective ways of observing the play of an individual child is to use a time-sampling chart (see the blank Observation record in Appendix 1).

The observer watches from a spot not too near the child but near enough to be able to note any verbal interaction the child may have with others. Using the second hand of a watch or a minute egg timer, the observer makes a tally mark at the end of each minute for a set period of time, e.g. five minutes, ten minutes, 20 minutes etc. If the child is on-task a tally mark may be put in the 'on-task' behaviour box – it does not matter what the task is – just as long as they are doing it! Other tally marks are made on the sheet whenever a different behaviour occurs, e.g. talking to other children or adults, wandering around, staring into space, invading another child's space.

A couple of short observations taken each day for a week can be very illuminating when you are concerned about a child's lack of progress or even if you are concerned about some of the activities you have on offer and are keen to know how (or if) they are providing a stimulating play experience.

This brief graphic Observation record completed for several short periods of time can sometimes provide a better overview of a child than a lengthy, continuous log of a child's movement around the play area (see the example Observation record completed for Jon Briggs in Appendix 1).

Observation once a week for a month or so can also help to detect patterns of a child's behaviour. Some children never seem to get into trouble but actually spend a large amount of time drifting, avoiding socialising with other children, avoiding particular activities, having good social interaction with peers but not with adults (or the other way round) or place too much reliance on the adults etc. This type of knowledge about children can be very valuable when meeting with parents/carers or planning for the next stage of their education.

APPENDIX 1

Recording pack

IEP – Ben

IEP – Milos

IEP – blank

Observation chart

Observation record – blank

Observation record – example

INDIVIDUAL EDUCATION PLAN

NAME: Ben	DoB:	PRE-SCHOOL:

PLAN NO: **ACTION/ACTION PLUS DATE:**

AREA(S) FOR DEVELOPMENT: Social and personal

TARGETS	STRATEGIES, RESOURCES, CONTRIBUTIONS
1 Ben will be able to complete an adult led task which lasts for two minutes.	Ben's key worker will play outside in the water tray alongside Ben while he puts pink dye into the tank (this usually takes two minutes to dissolve) and talk with him about the activity.
2 Ben will be able to put the tools used for digging by the garden and put them away every day for one week.	Ben's key worker will instruct him to do this at first with prompts if necessary and then gradually expect him to do this independently.
3	

TO BE ACHIEVED BY: **REVIEW DATE:**

SIGNATURES: SENCO: **PARENTS/GUARDIANS:**

REVIEW
1
2
3

FUTURE ACTION

SIGNATURES: SENCO: **PARENTS/GUARDIANS:**

INDIVIDUAL EDUCATION PLAN

NAME: *Milos*   **DoB:**   **PRE-SCHOOL:**

PLAN NO: **ACTION/ACTION PLUS DATE:**

AREA(S) FOR DEVELOPMENT: *Personal and social - turn taking*

TARGETS	STRATEGIES, RESOURCES, CONTRIBUTIONS
1 *Milos will be able to take turns appropriately during a game of picture lotto with an adult and one other child.*	*Milos's key worker will play the game with him and prompt and praise when necessary.*
2 *Milos will be able to wait in line to use the slide once per day.*	*Milos's key worker will be nearby to prompt and praise when necessary.*
3	

TO BE ACHIEVED BY: REVIEW DATE:
SIGNATURES: SENCO: PARENTS/GUARDIANS:

REVIEW

1

2

3

FUTURE ACTION

SIGNATURES: SENCO: PARENTS/GUARDIANS:

INDIVIDUAL EDUCATION PLAN

NAME:	DoB:	PRE-SCHOOL:

PLAN NO: ACTION/ACTION PLUS DATE:

AREA(S) FOR DEVELOPMENT:

TARGETS	STRATEGIES, RESOURCES, CONTRIBUTIONS
1	
2	
3	

TO BE ACHIEVED BY: REVIEW DATE:
SIGNATURES: SENCO: PARENTS/GUARDIANS:

REVIEW
1
2
3

FUTURE ACTION

SIGNATURES: SENCO: PARENTS/GUARDIANS:

OBSERVATION CHART

Name:		DoB:		Week commencing:	
Pre-school:					

Time	Mon	Tues	Wed	Thurs	Fri
9.00–9.15					
9.15–9.30					
9.30–9.45					
9.45–10.00					
10.00–10.15					
10.15–10.30					
10.30–10.45					
10.45–11.00					
11.00–11.15					
11.15–11.30					
11.30–11.45					
11.45–12.00					
12.00–12.15					
12.15–12.30					
12.30–12.45					
12.45–1.00					
1.00–1.15					
1.15–1.30					
1.30–1.45					
1.45–2.00					
2.00–2.15					
2.15–2.30					
2.30–2.45					
2.45–3.00					

On-task, happy, polite 5
On-task 4
Off-task/silent/refusing to reply 3
Off-task/verbally aggressive 2
Off-task/physically aggressive 1

OBSERVATION RECORD

Name:

Pre-school:

DoB: **Observed by:**

Date and time	On-task behaviour	Off-task behaviour – quiet	Off-task behaviour – disruptive					

Comments:

OBSERVATION RECORD

Name: Jon Briggs **DoB:** **Observed by:** Julie Andrews – Key worker

Pre-school: Sunnyside Pre-school

Date and time	On-task behaviour	Off-task behaviour – quiet	Off-task behaviour – disruptive						
			Snatching toy from another	Throwing sand/toys etc.	Running round the room	Shouting at another child	Shouting at adult	Ignoring instructions	Hiding in cloakroom
4/10/04									
10.00–10.10	卌	1	11	1	11	1	1	1111	
1.00–1.10 snack time	卌 1111	1						1	
2.20–2.30 tidying up	11		111	卌	111	11	111	卌	1

Comments: Jon has found it very hard to settle to any activity this morning. His most settled times were 1) when he played with Sanjit in the sand tray and 2) when he helped to pass around the fruit and drinks at snack time.

APPENDIX 2

Friends and family circle – blank

Friends and family circle – blank

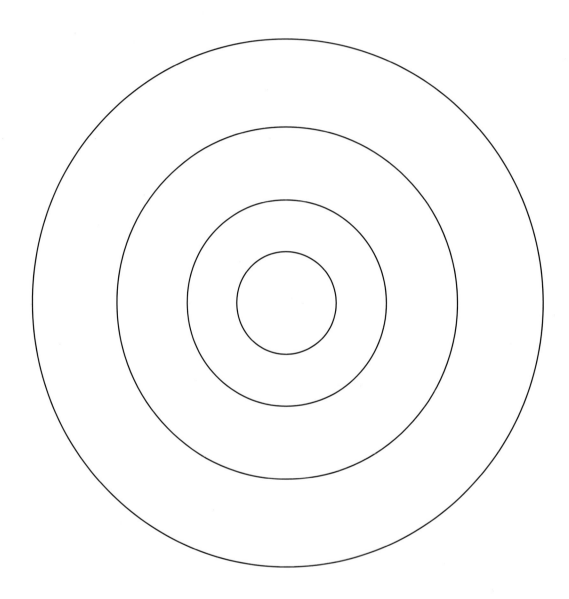

APPENDIX 3

Teddy bear climbing frame activity – blank

REFERENCES

Drake, J. (2005) *Planning Children's Play and Learning in the Foundation Stage* (2nd edn). London: David Fulton Publishers.

Glenn, A., Cousins, J. and Helps, A. (2004) *Behaviour in the Early Years*. London: David Fulton Publishers.

Glenn, A., Cousins, J. and Helps, A. (2005) *Removing Barriers to Learning in the Early Years*. London: David Fulton Publishers.

Qualifications and Curriculum Authority (QCA) (2000) *Curriculum Guidance for the Foundation Stage*. London: QCA.

FURTHER READING

Bilton, H. (2004) *Playing Outside: Activities, ideas and inspiration for the early years*. London: David Fulton Publishers.

Broadhead, P. (2003) *Early Years Play and Learning: Developing social skills and co-operation*. Oxford: RoutledgeFalmer.

Daly, M. (2005) *Developing the Whole Child: The importance of the emotional, social, moral and spiritual in early years education and care*. Lewiston: Edwin Meller Press.

Drifte, C. (2003) *Handbook for Pre-School SEN Provision*. London: David Fulton Publishers.

Green, S. (2004) *Creativity*. London: David Fulton Publishers.

Green, S. (2004) *Food and Cooking*. London: David Fulton Publishers.

Green, S. (2005) *Books, Stories and Puppets*. London: David Fulton Publishers.

Green, S. (2005) *Role Play*. London: David Fulton Publishers.

Green, S. and Harper, S. (2005) *Nature*. London: David Fulton Publishers.

Hewitson, C. (2004) *Festivals*. London: David Fulton Publishers.

Mortimer, H. (2000) *Developing Individual Behaviour Plans in Early Years*. Tamworth: NASEN.

Papatheodorou, T. (2005) *Behaviour Problems in the Early Years: Early identification and intervention*. Oxford: RoutledgeFalmer.

Tassoni, P. (2000) *Planning Play and the Early Years*. Oxford: Heinemann.

USEFUL ADDRESSES

The British Association of Art Therapists
24–27 Lion Street
London N1 9PD
Tel: 020 7686 4216
www.baat.org

The British Association of Play Therapists
31 Cedar Drive
Keynsham
Bristol BS31 2TY
Tel: 0117 9860390
www.bapt.info

Cruse Bereavement Care
Cruse House
126 Sheen Road
Richmond
Surrey TW9 1UR
Tel: 020 8939 9530
www.crusebereavementcare.org.uk

High/Scope UK
190–192 Maple Road
London SE20 8HT
Tel: 020 8676 0220
www.high-scope.org.uk

National Autistic Society
393 City Road
London EC1V 1NG
Tel: 020 7833 2299
Email: nas@nas.org.uk

Pre-school Learning Alliance
69 Kings Cross Road
London WC1X 9LL
Tel: 020 7833 0991
www.pre-school.org.uk

Smallwood Publishing Ltd
The Old Bakery
Charlton House
Dour Street
Dover
Kent CT16 1ED
Tel: 01304 226900
www.smallwood.co.uk